Capybaras

by Megan Borgert-Spaniol

BELLWETHER MEDIA · MINNEAPOLIS, MN

Note to Librarians, Teachers, and Parents:

Blastoff! Readers are carefully developed by literacy experts and combine standards-based content with developmentally appropriate text.

Level 1 provides the most support through repetition of high-frequency words, light text, predictable sentence patterns, and strong visual support.

Level 2 offers early readers a bit more challenge through varied simple sentences, increased text load, and less repetition of high-frequency words.

Level 3 advances early-fluent readers toward fluency through increased text and concept load, less reliance on visuals, longer sentences, and more literary language.

Level 4 builds reading stamina by providing more text per page, increased use of punctuation, greater variation in sentence patterns, and increasingly challenging vocabulary.

Level 5 encourages children to move from "learning to read" to "reading to learn" by providing even more text, varied writing styles, and less familiar topics.

Whichever book is right for your reader, Blastoff! Readers are the perfect books to build confidence and encourage a love of reading that will last a lifetime!

This edition first published in 2014 by Bellwether Media, Inc.

No part of this publication may be reproduced in whole or in part without written permission of the publisher. For information regarding permission, write to Bellwether Media, Inc., Attention: Permissions Department, 5357 Penn Avenue South, Minneapolis, MN 55419.

Library of Congress Cataloging-in-Publication Data

Borgert-Spaniol, Megan, 1989-
 Capybaras / by Megan Borgert-Spaniol.
  p. cm. – (Blastoff! readers. Animal safari)
 Summary: "Developed by literacy experts for students in kindergarten through grade three, this book introduces capybaras to young readers through leveled text and related photos"– Provided by publisher.
 Audience: K to grade 3.
 Includes bibliographical references and index.
 ISBN 978-1-60014-908-5 (hardcover : alk. paper)
 1. Capybara–Juvenile literature. I. Title. II. Series: Blastoff! readers. 1, Animal safari.
 QL737.R662B67 2014
 599.35'9–dc23
                                                          2013000882

Printed in the United States of America, North Mankato, MN.

Contents

What Are Capybaras?

Capybaras are the largest **rodents** in the world.

They live in ponds, **marshes**, and other wetlands. **Webbed feet** help them move in water.

webbed
feet

Capybaras stay cool in water or mud during the day. They **graze** when the sun goes down.

Eating

Capybaras eat grasses and **aquatic** plants. Their long, sharp teeth **grind** food.

Group Living

Capybaras live in groups. One male leads a group. Females care for the young.

Escaping Predators

Jaguars hunt capybaras. Large snakes called anacondas attack the young.

anaconda

Capybaras bark when **predators** are near. This warns others to look out.

A capybara
swims underwater
to escape danger.
It can stay there
for five minutes.

Then it pokes its
eyes and nose
out of the water.
Stay low, capybara!

Glossary

aquatic—living or growing in water

graze—to eat grasses and other plants

grind—to crush into smaller bits

marshes—wetlands with grasses and other plants

predators—animals that hunt other animals for food

rodents—small animals with front teeth that grow throughout life; rats, mice, and squirrels are types of rodents.

webbed feet—feet with thin skin that connects the toes

To Learn More

AT THE LIBRARY

Ganeri, Anita. *Capybara*. Chicago, Ill.: Heinemann Library, 2011.

Kalman, Bobbie. *Guinea Pigs and Other Rodents*. New York, N.Y.: Crabtree Pub. Co., 2006.

Lunis, Natalie. *Capybara: The World's Largest Rodent*. New York, N.Y.: Bearport Pub., 2010.

ON THE WEB
Learning more about capybaras is as easy as 1, 2, 3.

1. Go to www.factsurfer.com.

2. Enter "capybaras" into the search box.

3. Click the "Surf" button and you will see a list of related Web sites.

With factsurfer.com, finding more information is just a click away.

Index